Sports IN ACTION

Swimming

in Action

John Crossingham & Niki Walker

Illustrations by Bonna Rouse

🌳 **Crabtree Publishing Company**

www.crabtreebooks.com

Created by Bobbie Kalman

Dedicated by Niki Walker
For Jocelyn

Editor-in-Chief
Bobbie Kalman

Editorial director
Niki Walker

Writing team
John Crossingham
Niki Walker

Project editor
Rebecca Sjonger

Editors
Amanda Bishop
Kathryn Smithyman

Art director
Robert MacGregor

Design
Margaret Amy Reiach
Campbell Creative Services (cover)

Production coordinator
Heather Fitzpatrick

Photo research
Rebecca Sjonger
Jaimie Nathan

Special thanks to
Evelyn LeBoeuf, Kelly Bartok, Joshua Hales, Lindsey Potter
Karina Szczepanczyk, Paula Szczepanczyk, Morgan Washuta,
Jason Helstrom, Margie Lizzotti, Annette Partridge, Sarah Smith,
Eleanor Misener Aquatic Centre

Consultant
Tom Avischious, Programs & Services Director, USA Swimming

Photographs
Marc Crabtree: pages 10, 14 (bottom), 16, 20, 22, 27, 30,
    31 (top and bottom left)
Bobbie Kalman: page 14 (top)
Other images by Corbis Images, Digital Stock, PhotoDisc

Illustrations
All illustrations by Bonna Rouse

Digital prepress
Embassy Graphics

Printer
Worzalla Publishing Company

Crabtree Publishing Company

www.crabtreebooks.com   1-800-387-7650

Cataloging in Publication Data
Crossingham, John
    Swimming in action / John Crossingham & Niki Walker;
illustrations by Bonna Rouse.
    p. cm. -- (Sports in action)
Includes index.
This book describes the basic strokes, skills, competition, and important safety
information for the sport of swimming.
ISBN 0-7787-0331-2 (RLB) -- ISBN 0-7787-0315-7 (pbk.)
1. Swimming —Juvenile literature. [1. Swimming.] I. Walker, Niki. II. Rouse,
Bonna, ill. III. Title. IV. Series.
GV836.7.C76 2003
797.2'1--dc21
                                                                    LC 2002014304
                                                                    CIP

**Published in
the United States**
PMB 16A
350 Fifth Ave.
Suite 3308
New York, NY
10118

**Published
in Canada**
616 Welland Ave.,
St. Catharines,
Ontario, Canada
L2M 5V6

**Published in the
United Kingdom**
73 Lime Walk
Headington
Oxford
0X3 7AD
United Kingdom

**Published
in Australia**
386 Mt. Alexander Rd.,
Ascot Vale (Melbourne)
V1C 3032

Contents

What is swimming?

Swimming is one of the world's most popular activities. Some people swim for exercise. Others compete in races. Many people swim just for the fun of it! No matter what the reason, learning to swim is important. It could save your life!

A long history

People have been swimming for thousands of years, but swimming did not catch on as a sport until the 1800s. Competitive races started in England in 1837 and in the United States in 1888. In 1896, swimming was one of the sports at the first modern Olympics.

On the move

Over the years, people have developed many styles of swimming. **Strokes** are the fastest, easiest ways of moving through water. A stroke is a combination of body position, arm and leg movements, and breathing patterns. There are four competitive strokes—**freestyle**, **breaststroke**, **backstroke**, and **butterfly**. There are also two leisure strokes—**sidestroke** and **elementary backstroke**. You can read about them later in the book. When learning strokes, it is most important to feel when the movements are **efficient**—when they get you through the water quickly with the least amount of effort.

Learn in a pool

Many people enjoy swimming in **open water** such as lakes, ponds, and oceans, but open water can be dangerous. It often has a **current**, which is quickly flowing water. Some currents are so strong that they overpower swimmers and pull them far away from land. Open water may also have **undercurrents**, which are hidden under the surface. These currents can drag swimmers underwater. Never swim in open water without adult supervision. This book has tips for learning to swim in a pool.

Welcome to the pool

Swimming pools come in all shapes and sizes, but most public pools are rectangular, such as the one shown right. They usually have sloping bottoms, so that one end is deeper than the other. There are indoor and outdoor pools. **Aboveground** pools sit on top of the ground. Most pools, however, are **in-ground**. An in-ground pool is dug into the ground.

DEEP END

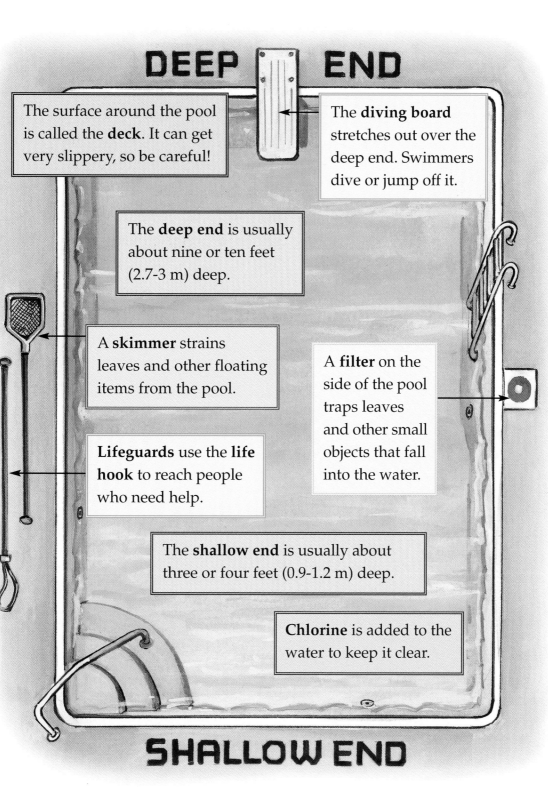

The surface around the pool is called the **deck**. It can get very slippery, so be careful!

The **diving board** stretches out over the deep end. Swimmers dive or jump off it.

The **deep end** is usually about nine or ten feet (2.7-3 m) deep.

A **skimmer** strains leaves and other floating items from the pool.

A **filter** on the side of the pool traps leaves and other small objects that fall into the water.

Lifeguards use the **life hook** to reach people who need help.

The **shallow end** is usually about three or four feet (0.9-1.2 m) deep.

Chlorine is added to the water to keep it clear.

SHALLOW END

Pool rules and safety

A good time at the pool can be ruined by an accident. Whether you're at a public pool or in a friend's back yard, make sure an adult who can swim is watching you. The adult should also know **first aid** and how to perform **CPR**, which stands for **cardiopulmonary resuscitation**. CPR is used when a person has had an accident and is not breathing. This life-saving technique can help the person begin to breathe again.

Take a CPR course!

It is a good idea for you to learn CPR and first aid. Take a course led by a qualified instructor. The Red Cross Society and most local fitness centers offer these courses.

There should always be at least one lifeguard on duty at a public pool. A lifeguard helps swimmers when they need assistance and makes sure everyone in and around the pool is playing safely. Always obey lifeguards!

Keep it safe!

No matter where you swim, there are rules to help prevent accidents and keep swimmers safe. At a public pool, these rules are posted for you. Make sure you know the rules before getting into the water, and always obey them.

Look before you leap! Never jump into the water near other swimmers. You could hit someone by accident.

*Never **dunk** another swimmer! Holding people under the water is dangerous because they might run out of breath.*

Never shove people into the pool! They could hurt themselves by hitting the water the wrong way, or they could fall onto another swimmer.

Never run on the deck! It is usually wet, which makes it slippery.

The essentials

To go swimming, you do not need a lot of equipment. In fact, you usually don't need more than a swimsuit and a towel. If you're at an outdoor pool, always wear a strong sunscreen, too. It should be waterproof and have an **SPF**, or sun protection factor, of 30 or higher.

Besides the basics, there are other types of swimming equipment you can buy. Some gear is designed to make you more **streamlined**. Streamlined objects move smoothly through water. Other equipment just makes swimming more fun.

Swimsuits

There are many styles of swimsuits. It is important to find a suit that is comfortable, no matter how you move in it. Whatever type of suit you wear, always rinse it out after swimming in a pool. Chlorine damages the fabric and makes your suit wear out faster.

Look out below!

Goggles allow you to see clearly underwater. They are especially useful in pools if chemicals bother your eyes.

Frog feet

Wide rubber **fins** slip over your feet. They give you more kicking power and make swimming faster and easier. When you are learning to swim, wearing fins is a great way to improve your kicking style.

*A **swimming cap** is a snug rubber hat that keeps long hair tucked out of the way.*

*Some swimmers wear **nose plugs** to keep water from going up their noses as they move through the water.*

Breathing easy

A **diving mask** helps you see underwater. Unlike goggles, a mask covers your nose. A **snorkel** sticks up above the water's surface and allows you to breathe without having to lift your face out of the water.

Warming up

Swimming is a sport that uses your entire body. It is important to perform some stretches before you hit the water. Stretching warms up your muscles, so you are less likely to pull or strain them. Concentrate on stretches for your legs, arms, and neck. These pages have some good examples of swimming stretches.

Ankle stretch

Sit on the ground with one leg straight in front of you. Bend your other leg so that you can grab your foot. Gently move it in circles. When you have done ten circles, do ten more in the other direction. Change legs.

Arm circles

Stand with your feet shoulder-width apart. Stretch your arms out to the sides and swing them in giant circles. Make the motions smaller and smaller until your arms are moving in tiny circles straight out to your sides. Now swing them in the opposite direction, starting with small circles and finishing with large circles.

Toe touches

Stand with your feet slightly apart and your knees slightly bent. Bend at the waist and try to touch your toes. Without straightening up, bring your left hand across and touch the toes on your right foot. Hold the stretch for a count of ten. Now touch your left toes with your right hand. Repeat ten times.

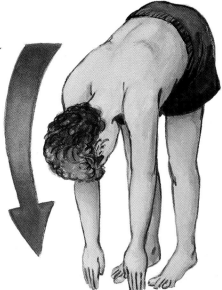

Quadriceps stretch

Stand on your right foot and use your right hand to support yourself against a wall. Bring your left foot up behind you until you can grab it with your left hand. Pull gently until you feel the front of your leg stretch. Hold the stretch for a count of ten and then switch legs.

Neck circles

It's easy to hurt your neck, so be careful when you do this stretch. Tilt your head forward so that your chin points at your chest. Slowly move your head toward one shoulder and then the other. Never roll your head backward or farther than feels comfortable.

Getting wet

It's normal to feel nervous in the water when you're learning how to swim. Before you even think of learning strokes, it is important that you spend time in a pool, just getting used to the water and how your body moves in it. Doing so will help you build confidence. Start out in the shallow end of the pool and always have an adult close by.

Floating

Learning how to float is the first step in learning how to swim. In the shallow end, lie on your back on the surface of the water. Get an adult to place both hands under your shoulder blades. Breathe slowly and deeply. Notice how your body floats more easily when your lungs are full of air. Don't worry if your legs and **torso** hang down instead of floating. Everyone floats differently. Once you're comfortable floating on your back, hold your breath and try floating on your front with your face in the water. Extending your arms will help you float. Roll from your front to your back and then return to your front.

Controlled breathing

Learning to breathe properly in the water is an important step in learning to swim. You don't have to be able to hold your breath for long. You just have to control when you inhale and exhale. Doing so will help you later, when you start learning strokes. To practice controlling your breath, try **bobbing**. Hold on to the edge of the pool, take a deep breath, and gradually sink underwater. Slowly let out all the air by blowing bubbles through your mouth and nose. Return to the surface. When your mouth is above the water, take a deep breath and sink again. Keep bobbing until you don't even have to think about when to inhale and exhale.

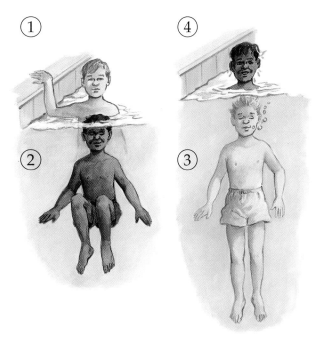

Bobbing can help if you ever find yourself in water that is too deep for you. Instead of panicking, simply bob between the surface and the bottom. Each time you go down, kick off the bottom in the direction of shallow water.

Treading

When you are comfortable floating on your back, try **treading** water. Treading is like jogging on the spot. Try it where you can touch the pool's bottom without the water going above your shoulders. Start by moving your hands as if you're spreading peanut butter on two slices of bread at the same time. Turn your hands so that the cupped part is always "pushing" against the water. Now bring your knees up toward your chest and pedal as though you're riding a bike.

Treading water helps keep your head above the surface. Move your legs as if you're pedaling a bike.

Easy does it!

Once you feel comfortable in the water, you're ready to try some easy ways of getting around. The moves shown here combine floating with simple arm movements and kicks that push against the water. Remember, the more streamlined you make your body, the faster and easier you'll move.

Gliding

Gliding is simply floating in motion. To glide, push off the wall of the pool with your feet and stretch out your arms and legs. Make your body as streamlined as possible so you glide farther before slowing down. You can try gliding with your arms against your sides, too. Once you master gliding on your front, roll over and try it on your back.

Sculling

Some people have an easier time floating than others do. If your legs and torso sink when you float on your back, you can **scull** to keep your body at the surface. Sculling uses gentle movements of your hands in the water. Your hands push away from your hips and then back toward them in a continuous figure-eight motion. You can also use sculling to move around.

To glide well, imagine that your body is a torpedo and make it as streamlined as you can.

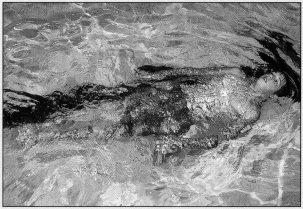

Pointing your fingers down when sculling moves you feet first. Pointing them up moves you headfirst.

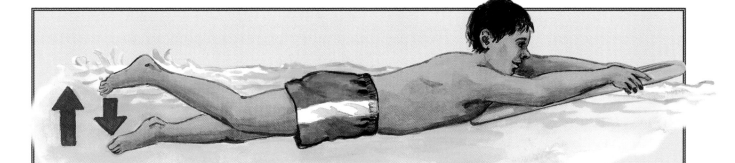

*The **flutter kick**, shown here, uses an alternating motion—one foot moves down while the other moves up.*

Kick it!

Kicking is one of the easiest ways to **propel**, or move, yourself through the water. Your legs can create a lot of power! Practice kicking by holding a flutter board, "noodle," or other floating device under your chest. If you don't have a floating device, hold on to the pool's edge and straighten your body behind you.

As you kick, keep your legs straight but relaxed and your ankles loose. Make your kicks smooth and even. Remember, good kicking is not a water-spraying contest! You get more power from your legs if your ankles are just below the surface of the water and your feet just break the surface.

Doggin' it

The **front paddle**, or "dog paddle," is a good way for beginners to move in water. You will stop doing this paddle as you learn to swim strokes, but it will help you build confidence in the meantime.

To do the front paddle, hold your hands so the palms face your feet. Move your hands in forward circles as though you are pedaling with them. Kick your feet back and forth. Hold your head above water.

Swimming freestyle

Once you're able to control your breathing and feel comfortable gliding and paddling, you're ready to try your first stroke—the freestyle, or **front crawl**. The freestyle is the fastest and most common stroke. It is most effective if you don't lift your head out of the water to breathe. Doing so slows you down. You must learn to turn your head and quickly take a breath while one arm is at your hip and the other is reaching forward underwater. Practice timing your breathing with your arm movements while standing in the shallow end.

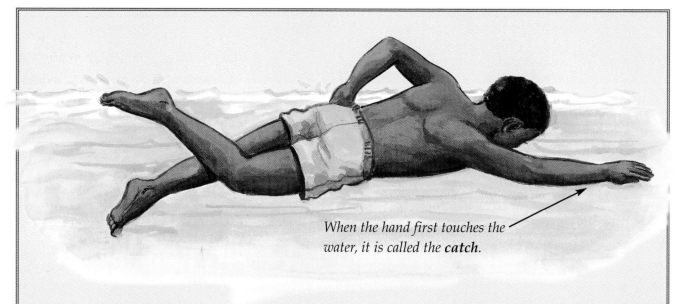

When the hand first touches the water, it is called the **catch**.

1. Push off the edge of the pool in a streamlined position with both arms out in front (see page 16). When you start to slow down, get moving with a flutter kick. Stretch your right arm forward while you draw your left arm back through the water. Now you are ready to start the stroke.

2. Bend your right arm slightly as it enters the water. Imagine that you are using your right hand to grab the water and push it behind you. Meanwhile, lift your left arm out of the water behind you and move it forward.

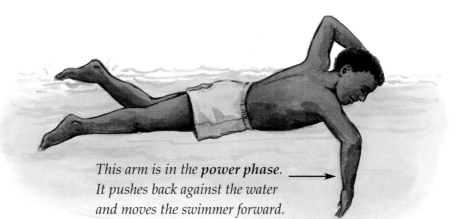

This arm is in the **power phase**. It pushes back against the water and moves the swimmer forward.

There is no glide in the front crawl. Your arms and legs are always moving.

3. By the time your left arm enters the water, your right arm is coming out of the water near your hip. Your body rolls slightly as your arm lifts. Now is the perfect time to take a breath, since your face is out of the water!

Now this arm is in the **recovery phase**. It is on its way back to the water to start another power phase.

4. Your right arm moves through the air as your left arm pushes through the water. Remember to keep kicking your legs up and down. Try to keep them fairly straight and kick from your hips instead of your knees.

19

Backstrokes

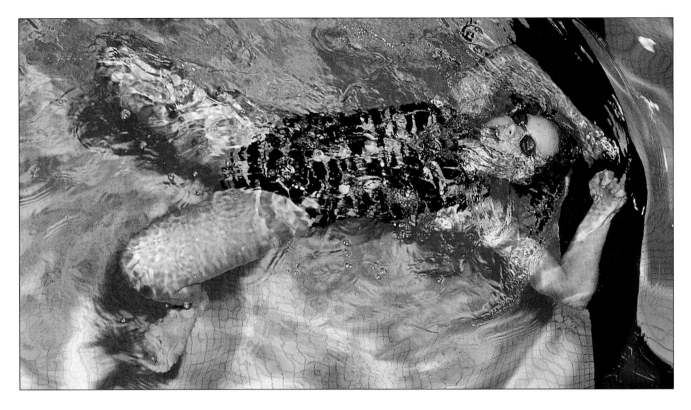

There are two types of backstrokes: the **elementary backstroke** and the **backstroke**. You may find backstrokes easier to learn than the freestyle, since your face is out of the water and you can take a breath whenever you need to.

It's elementary

The elementary backstroke is easy to do. It's a great stroke to use just for fun or when you feel tired. It's slower than other strokes, but it also takes little effort. To do the elementary backstroke, start by floating on your back. Slide your hands up along your sides to your ears. Turn your hands outward and cup them slightly. Without taking your hands out of the water, move them up as far as the top of your head. Straighten your arms slightly and move your hands out to the side. Push your hands through the water toward your hips, so your arms make large, curving motions. Now you're ready to add the kick. The kick, called a **whip kick**, is shown above.

The backstroke

To do the backstroke, add alternating arm movements to a flutter kick. While one arm is out of the water, the other is "pulling" you through it.

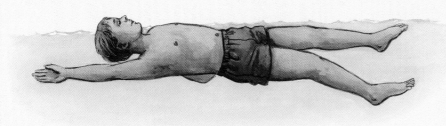

1. Float on your back and start doing a flutter kick. Lift your right hand out of the water. Leading with your pinky finger, swing your arm straight above your head and drop it into the water. Dip your right shoulder down.

2. When your right hand is fully in the water, bend your elbow and push against the water with your palm. At the same time, lift your left arm out of the water.

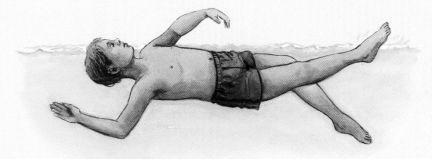

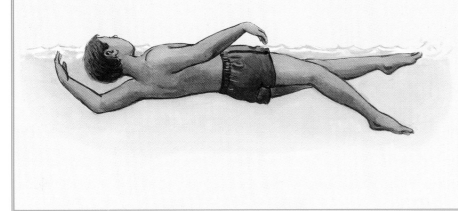

3. Keep pushing your right hand through the water. Start rotating your body to the other side and straighten your left arm. Reach it above your head and into the water. Try to avoid a "catch-up," where one arm moves faster than the other and both hands end up at your hips together.

The breaststroke

In the breaststroke, you don't use alternating movements, as in the freestyle. Instead, both your arms move together and so do your legs.

Your arms and legs never leave the water. The breaststroke is not as fast as the freestyle, but it allows you to look ahead as you swim.

The breaststroke is a good one to use when you swim underwater because you can easily look ahead and around you without your arms getting in the way.

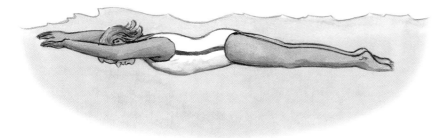

1. Begin in a streamlined position, with your arms pointing forward and your legs straight behind you. Place your face in the water.

2. Sweep your arms out to the side, bend them at your elbows, and point your hands down. At the same time, begin lifting your legs upward. Start raising your head and shoulders out of the water.

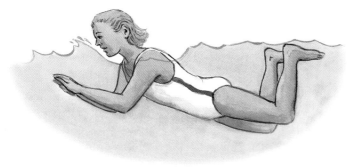

3. Raise your head and shoulders above the surface and take a breath. Keep your elbows bent and bring your hands together. Bend your knees and angle your hips down in the water. Lift up your lower legs so that the bottoms of your feet are just under the surface. Push your body forward with the whip kick.

4. When your kick is done, bring your legs back together in a streamlined position. Straighten your arms in front of you with your hands together. Glide for a moment and then repeat the stroke.

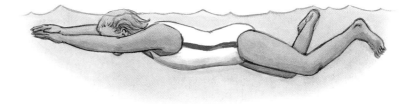

The sidestroke

The sidestroke is a relaxed stroke. Breathing is easy, since your nose and mouth are always out of the water. The sidestroke uses the **scissor kick**, which has two parts—a kick and a glide. The "scissor" part of the kick propels you forward. The stronger your kick, the more time you have to glide.

This arm is called the upper arm since the shoulder is slightly ahead of the other one. The other arm is the lower arm.

①

②

③

1. Glide on your side. Your head, back, and legs are in a line, and your toes are pointed. Stretch one arm above your head, leaving the other at your side.

2. Imagine that you are moving your upper arm to pick an apple above your head and then passing the "apple" to your lower hand, at your waist. Bend the elbow of your lower arm and pull your hand up toward your head. Stop when your hand is at the top of your chest. As you move your arms, pull your heels toward your bottom. Keep your hips forward.

3. Now move your lower hand back to your hip. As your lower arm moves down, your upper arm moves up. Return both arms to their starting positions. Flex your feet and straighten your legs as you push your top leg forward while pushing your bottom leg backward. Quickly close your legs like the blades of scissors, and return to the glide position.

The butterfly

The butterfly stroke, shown right, is very difficult. It requires more energy than other strokes do. If you like a challenge, however, you can practice it once you're comfortable with the other strokes. Some swimmers have to practice a lot before they get the timing of the stroke right.

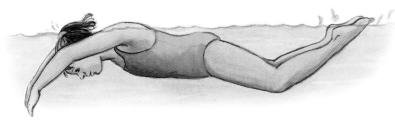

1. Bend your elbows slightly and drive your arms into the water. As your arms come down, kick up once with your legs. Move your arms down through the water and under your body. Push the water with your palms.

2. As your arms reach your thighs, start to pull your legs down. Raise your shoulders and head out of the water. Take a quick breath before you start raising your arms out of the water.

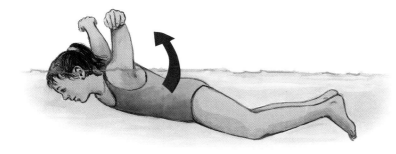

3. When your arms are fully above the water, your head and shoulders begin to dip back down into the water. Drive your arms into the water again and kick up with your legs.

Take the plunge

Be sure the pool is clear of people before you jump in!

Jumping into the pool can be as much fun as swimming! The most important part of jumping is to be safe. Never jump or **dive** into the shallow end. A dive is a headfirst jump into the pool. There are a lot of ways to jump into water, but try not to **belly flop**, or hit the water on your stomach. That hurts!

A cannonball makes a big splash! When you jump, curl into a ball and grab your knees.

To keep your head above water when you jump into the pool, hold your arms out to the sides, bend your knees, and take a big step forward into the water. Keep one leg ahead of the other and your knees bent as you hit the water. Your outstretched arms and legs help keep your head and shoulders above the surface.

Going in headfirst

You have to be very careful when diving, or you could hit your head on the bottom of the pool and seriously hurt yourself. Dive only when you can see the bottom of the pool and are sure that the water is at least eight feet (2.4 m) deep. Always dive with your arms in front of your head, so your fingers enter the water first.

The shallow dive

You should always learn to dive with a qualified instructor. Always practice in deep, clear water. There are many types of dives, but the **shallow dive** is good for beginners. Start from a sitting or kneeling position at the side of the pool. Don't even think of trying a standing shallow dive, shown right, until you're totally comfortable!

To do a standing shallow dive, curl your toes over the edge of the diving board and bend your knees. Bend forward at the waist. Lean far forward and swing both arms ahead. Bring your arms together and tuck your head down. At the same time, give a hard push up and forward with your legs. Straighten your legs and point your toes. Your hands enter the water first, followed by your arms and head.

Racing

Swimming races can be held outdoors or in indoor pools. In **open-water races**, people swim in lakes or oceans. These races are often part of larger events called **triathlons**. Athletes competing in a triathlon swim, run, and cycle outdoors. At the Olympics, swimmers compete in a pool that is 164 feet (50 m) long, but most pools are 25 yards (23 m) long. Swimmers can compete as individuals or as part of a team.

Each **event**, or race, is named for the length of the race and the type of stroke used. For example, the 100 meter backstroke and 400 meter freestyle are two types of swimming events. The **medley** is the only event in which more than one stroke is used. Racers swim a length of the butterfly, a length of the backstroke, a length of the breaststroke, and a length of the freestyle.

*Racers must stay inside their lanes. If they leave their lanes, they are **disqualified**, or forced to leave the race.*

Go team, go!

Team competitions happen in two ways. In some competitions, each member of a team swims an individual race. Swimmers earn points based on either their times or their ranking, and the team with the most points wins. Teams also have **relay** races, such as the 4 x 100 freestyle. In this race, the "4" stands for the number of swimmers on each team, and the "100" is the number of yards or meters each team member swims. As soon as the first member swims the distance, the second one starts, and so on.

Strong start

A race starts with a countdown that is called out by an official or signaled by a machine. If a racer dives before the countdown ends, it is a **false start**. Two false starts disqualify a racer. At the end of the countdown, racers enter the water with shallow dives and glide just below the surface to start their strokes.

Turn it around

Racers have to turn at the end of their lanes and come back. Turns must be done well, or a racer loses valuable time. Racers do not have much room to turn in their narrow lanes. In freestyle races, the turn is like an underwater somersault.

An open-water race can have hundreds of athletes swimming at once.

*Swimmers start the race on platforms called **blocks**. They wait for the signal and then spring forward using their legs.*

Pool games

A swimming pool is a great place for games—as long as you remember to play safely! There are many pool games, and most require little or no extra equipment. You can even make up your own games with your friends. These pages have some ideas to get the fun started.

Marco Polo

This classic pool game is best played with at least three people. One person is selected as "*it*," and this player has to keep his or her eyes closed. *It* then has to find and touch one of the other players. *It* shouts, "Marco!" The other players must reply, "Polo!" *It* follows the sounds of their voices and tries to tag one of the other players. The tagged player becomes the new *it*.

Go deep!

To practice swimming underwater, drop objects along the bottom of the pool. Make sure the items will sink and are not breakable! With a friend, take turns diving down for the objects. Time each other to see who can get back to the surface of the water more quickly.

Play ball!

Air-filled balls won't sink, so they are great for the pool. You can play all kinds of games with them, such as basketball. Set up flutter boards on the deck at either end of the pool and try to knock them over with the ball.

Water polo

Water polo is an Olympic sport for both men and women. Water polo is like soccer in a pool, but the players pass and shoot the ball with their hands instead of their feet. Players have to be in great shape to be able to pass and catch the ball while swimming around their opponents.

Glossary

Note: Boldfaced words that are defined in the book may not appear in the glossary.

backstroke A stroke with arms and legs in continuous motion, performed on the back with the face out of the water

breaststroke A gliding stroke performed facedown in the water

butterfly An energetic stroke that imitates a butterfly's flapping wings

chlorine A chemical used to keep pool water clear and free of bacteria

CPR Cardiopulmonary resuscitation, or the process of helping someone who is not breathing or whose heart has stopped beating

diving board A springy board from which swimmers jump or dive

elementary backstroke A gliding stroke performed on the back with the face out of the water

first aid The treatment of a wounded or sick person before medical help arrives

freestyle A stroke with arms and legs in continuous motion, performed facedown in the water

front crawl Another name for the freestyle

medley A swimming event in which more than one stroke is used—usually the butterfly, backstroke, breaststroke, and freestyle

relay A race with several stages, each stage performed by a different team member

shallow dive A dive that sends the swimmer just below the surface of the water

sidestroke A stroke performed with the body turned sideways in the water

streamlined Describing a sleek shape

torso The part of the human body to which arms, legs, and a head are attached

whip kick A kick in which the swimmer brings the heels toward the backside, separates the knees and heels, and then rotates the feet outward and downward until the feet and ankles touch

Index

2 3 4 5 6 7 8 9 0   Printed in the U.S.A.   2 1 0 9 8 7 6 5 4